ISAIAH'S CLOSING ARGUMENTS

ISAIAH'S CLOSING ARGUMENTS
A New Translation

Laurance Wieder

Foreword by Blaire A. French

HIGH
LAND
BOOKS

ACKNOWLEDGMENTS

For this translation of Isaiah, I am indebted to my friend and collaborator Blaire French, who proved my English against the original text and never hesitated to tell me,

"Larry, the Hebrew doesn't say that."

Thanks also to Rabbi Dan Alexander, who invited me to read the English *Haftarah* on Yom Kippur, some years back.

Finally, thank you to my fellow members of the traditional Shabbat morning minyan at Congregation Beth Israel in Charlottesville, Virginia.

Copyright © 2019
Laurance Wieder
Foreword copyright © 2019
Blaire A. French
All rights reserved

HIGH
LAND
BOOKS

ISBN: 978-1-7330907-0-4

COVER DESIGN: **Matthew Morse**/ heymatthew.com
COVER ART: *The Prophet Isaiah*, Maestro de Becerril, *circa* 1525
Heritage Image Partnership Ltd. / Alamy Stock Photo

TABLE OF CONTENTS

FOREWORD 7
TO THE READER 11
OPENINGS 15
   ISAIAH 42:5-43:10 17
   ISAIAH 54:1-55:5 22
   ISAIAH 40:27-41:16 26
   ISAIAH 27:6-28:13 & 29:22-23 29
   ISAIAH 6:1-7:6 & 9:5-6 32
   ISAIAH 43:21-44:23 35
   ISAIAH 1:1-27 40
CONSOLATIONS 45
   ISAIAH 40:1-26 47
   ISAIAH 49:14-51:3 51
   ISAIAH 54:11-55:5 56
   ISAIAH 51:12-52:12 58
   ISAIAH 54:1-10 62
   ISAIAH 60:1-22 64
   ISAIAH 61:10-63:9 68
OCCASIONS 75
   ISAIAH 58:1-14 77
   ISAIAH 10:32-12:6 80
   ISAIAH 55:6-56:8 84
   ISAIAH 66:1-24 87
SOURCES 93

FOREWORD

It would begin with an email, subject heading:

Any time for Izzy?

That was when I knew that Larry Wieder had completed another translation of Isaiah.

At the appointed hour I'd arrive at Larry's house, follow him to the back study, and take my seat on a small couch. Larry sat at his desk, his marvelous library of foundational Jewish literature lining the bookcase behind him. I would have in my hand the Hebrew text for the *Haftarah* we were about to consider. Then Larry would read his translation while I checked him against the original.

It was the best job in the world.

Larry and I met in a Biblical Hebrew class at the University of Virginia. Our true friendship, however, took root at the synagogue. Several years ago, on Yom Kippur, he read his English translation of Isaiah 58:1-14, the *Haftarah* for the morning service. By then I was a regular *ḥazzan* (cantor) for our lay-led minyan, and an adjunct lecturer in Biblical Hebrew at UVa. As I sat in the sanctuary with my fellow congregants, I felt as if I were hearing the *Haftarah* for the first time. There was an urgency and vividness that other standard translations lacked. When I looked at the Hebrew, I saw that Larry had arrived at a striking and novel, though entirely defensible, alternative to the usual translation. Thus, when God defines what it means to fast, He does not say, "No, this is the fast I desire: To unlock fetters of wickedness...to untie the cords of the yoke...to let the oppressed go free...to break off every yoke...to share your bread with the hungry... to take the wretched poor into your home... to clothe him [the naked one]" (The Jewish Publication Society translation). Rather, God says:

> No. This is the fast I require:
> Strike off the chains of injustice.
> Cut loose the bonds of oppression.
> Set the yoked people free.
> You must break every yoke, every chain.
> No. More.
> Share your bread with the hungry.
> Bring the homeless poor into your house.
> When you see naked ones, clothe them.
> Do not hide from your own flesh and blood.

I was not the only congregant who was moved that morning. Larry's rendering of this *Haftarah* has been part of the Yom Kippur service in Congregation Beth Israel of Charlottesville, Virginia ever since.

I began my modest part in helping him not long afterwards. My usual practice was to interrupt if I wanted to discuss the verse at hand. Then, once deliberations were over, Larry would carry on until the next interruption. The process was never routine, however. I remember well the day Larry presented his version of the Isaiah *Haftarah* that follows the reading of Genesis 6:9-11:32 (Isaiah 54:1-55:5). We were about halfway through when he read to me these words of God to Israel:

> You poor, heart-battered, unconsoled:
> See, I set your walkways with mosaics,

> and founded you on sapphires,
> pile rubies atop your walls,
> hew gates from flaming garnet,
> mark all your borders with desire's stones,
> so all your children learn the Name
> and know great peace.

I was so struck by the beauty and freshness of these lines that I made him stop. There was nothing to discuss. I just wanted a moment to take it all in.

With every meeting I became more and more conscious of Larry's affinity with Isaiah. Part of this connection stems from the fact that Larry is himself a poet and thus has a unique perspective on Isaiah's artistry. But part of it springs from something that is even harder to attain: kinship with ancient inspiration and imagination.

With the publication of *Isaiah's Closing Arguments,* others also may now hear Isaiah as Larry hears him. I will always be grateful that I was among the first to receive this gift.

—Blaire A. French
May 13, 2019

TO THE READER

In this world, in synagogues on every Sabbath morning, one *parshah* or portion from the fifty-four chapters of Moses' books is read aloud from the Torah scroll in the presence of a minyan of at least ten worshippers.

Removed from the ark—a curtained cabinet behind the raised platform or *bimah*—the Torah is carried through the sanctuary accompanied by chanted psalms, taken back to the *bimah*, and placed upon the reader's table facing the congregation. Returned to its place at the conclusion of the Torah service by the way it came, the scroll again passes among the congregants to a song of David. Written without error by a scribe's hand, the Torah scroll is the ritual, intellectual, dramatic, and moral center of the morning service.

Our traditional, lay-led congregation features a *d'var torah* or torah talk prepared by a member of the minyan that precedes the prescribed reading. After the day's Torah portion is read, and before the sacred scroll is returned to its ark, another participant chants the *Haftarah* (plural: *Haftorot*)—a valediction to Moses' words taken from the Hebrew Prophets. Fourteen of these pointed farewells to the scroll are drawn from Isaiah.

Isaiah's verses conclude readings from the three beginnings recorded in Genesis: the creation itself, Noah's flood, and God's call to Abraham. The prophet's poems punctuate two chapters of Exodus: the story of Moses, and the giving of the Ten Commandments. A sixth *Haftarah* accompanies the first chapter of Leviticus, and a seventh closes the opening of the second Torah, Deuteronomy.

Seven of Isaiah's orations, the *Haftorot* of Consolation, serve as counterpoint to the final portions of Moses' somber recapitulation of the Law, Israel's journey out of Egypt through the Wilderness, blessings and curses, and their teacher's account of his own death.

Four more poems by the prophet are read out at special services: instruction to those assembled on Yom Kippur; a prophecy for the last day of Passover; a prayer for God's house on *Shabbat Ḥazon*—the Sabbath before *Tisha B'Av*—which marks the destruction of both the First Temple and the Second; and lastly, a proclamation of *Rosh Ḥodesh*—the New Moon—when it falls on the Sabbath.

Unlike my native English, Biblical Hebrew verbs mark time through context, not by formed tenses. Verbs in the Torah, the Prophets and the Writings indicate two states of action: complete—that is, of the past—and the incomplete. The incomplete comprehends both the elusive living present, and the imagined future.

Isaiah, the prophet of hope, sings mostly in the incomplete of things that we might hear, and so amend, and understand. Against the present failures of imagination, and of the often deaf-and-blind self, Isaiah espouses a yet-to-be-realized time of justice and clarity.

As I made these translations, I heard the Hebrew poet's voice—immediate and piercing—and rendered its tone and passion in the language of my understanding. Some passages of Isaiah's prophecies refer to current events, names and places so blurred by time that it's hard to be stirred by what then must have buzzed. In some instances, I substituted the Hebrew Lexicon definition of a proper noun—for example, "upright one" in place of Jeshurun. To explicate a timeless conflict, Aram and Ephraim become Syria and the Northern Kingdom

Other words sound vexed to my ear. "Savior" has sectarian overtones; "purify" and "purity" seem priestly and inward; "messiah" is often construed as something other than what the Hebrew means. To ground the discourse, this Isaiah finds in the creator and redeemer a near kinsman, who clarifies the human heart and accepts sincerity and understanding as forms of sacrifice and worship.

—Laurance Wieder

OPENINGS
Genesis, Exodus, Leviticus, Deuteronomy

ISAIAH 42:5-43:10
for BERE'SHIT/בראשית—Genesis 1:1-6:8

"So," said God, the LORD
  who created the sky and unfurled it,
    spread out the earth and all that springs from it,
  gives breath to the people on it
    and spirit to those who walk there:
"I, the One, called you for justice
    and strengthened your hand;
I keep you and give you
  as a covenant people, as a light to nations,
    to open blind eyes,
      to deliver the chained from a dungeon,
    from the prison house sitting in darkness.
I, the LORD, that is my name.
  My glory I give to no other,
    nor my sung praises to carved images.
The first things—see—have come to pass.
  New things I now declare:
before they spring up
    I make you hear them."

  Sing a new song to the LORD.
    Praise him from the end of the earth,
you who sail the sea, and all that lives in it,
    by coasts and on islands.
Wilderness and cities raise their voice,
    people of the dark walled towns;

rock dwellers sing loud for joy,
    shout from the mountaintops.
They fashion glory to the LORD,
    tell his praise in every country.
The LORD goes forth as a mighty man;
    like a man of war stirs passion
He cries out. More, he roars;
    he lords it over his enemies.

Of old, I kept silent,
    plowed my furrow, held back.
Now I groan, like a woman in labor
    gasps and pants at once:
I waste mountains and hills,
    wither all their grasses,
make rivers bare land
    and dry up the marshes.
I bring the blind along an unknown way,
    lead them by paths they did not know;
I make darkness light before them,
    the crooked, plain.
These things
    I do, and without fail.
They turn back, ashamed
    who trust in carved images,
Who say to molten idols,
    "You: our gods."

You deaf: hear.
　　You blind: look, to see.
Who is blind, but my servant?
　　Who deaf as the messenger I send?
Who so blind as one at peace,
　　and blind as a servant of the LORD?
Seeing much, yet you do not observe;
　　opening ears, but he hears not.
The LORD delights for his justice's sake;
　　he magnifies the Law, and elevates.
But this, a people spoiled, plundered,
Trapped in holes, all
　　clapped in prison houses:
fallen prey, with no deliverer;
　　the spoil, and no one says "Return."

Who among you gives ear to this?
Who attends and hears what is to come?
Who gave Jacob for spoil,
　　and Israel to plunderers?
The LORD, no?
　　Him we sinned against.
They did not walk in his ways;
　　nor did they listen to his law.
Furious, God turned a burning face to them:
fierce battle scorched his every side—
　　he did not learn;
consumed by anger, he took it not to heart.

"But now," said the LORD your Creator, "Jacob,"
    (He who formed you, Israel):
    "fear not, I have redeemed you.
        I called you by name; you are mine.
    When you pass over waters, I am with you;
        rivers will not overwhelm you.
    When you walk through fire, you will not scorch;
        flame will not consume you.
    For I Am—the LORD your God,
        the holy One of Israel—your rescue.
    I gave Egypt for your ransom,
        took Cush and his son's lands instead of you.
    Since you are precious in my sight,
        you are honored and I love you—
    so I offered mankind in exchange for you,
        and for your selves, gave nations.
    Fear not, for I am with you.

"From the east I bring your seed,
    and from the west, I gather you together.
I say to the north, 'Give up,'
    and to the south, 'Do not keep back.'
Bring in my sons from distant lands,
    my daughters from the ends of the earth.
All those called by my name
    I created for my glory:
        them I formed, I made.

"Bring forth the blind with eyes,
    the deaf with ears.
Assemble all the nations together,
    gathered as a people.
Who among them can make this known,
    serve as our herald of first things?
Let them appoint their witnesses, be justified;
    let them hear, and answer: 'Truth.'

"You are my witnesses"—
        the One says—
"and my servant I have chosen,
    so that you may know and trust me
        and understand that I am He.
Before me, no God was formed
    and none will after me."

ISAIAH 54:1-55:5
for NOAH/נח—Genesis 6:9-11:32

Sing, you barren, childless.
    Break into song, cry out
        who have not borne.
    (The children of abandoned wives
        outnumber children of the married.)

The LORD said:
    Enlarge your nomad campground, stretch
        the curtains of your dwelling out.
    Don't stint: extend your tent stays,
        reinforce your stakes.
    For right and left you burst forth,
        and your offspring inherits
        nations, and peoples desolate cities.
    Don't fear, don't feel ashamed,
        nor be confused, nor shoulder blame.
    Forget your youthful shame,
        your widows' scorn recall no more.
    For your husband is your Maker—
        The LORD of Hosts his name—
and your redeemer, the holy One of Israel,
        called God of all the earth.

For, though a woman forsaken,
    a tortured spirit, the LORD called you.
Although a young wife cast aside,

OPENINGS

    your God said:
        In a small moment I forsook you,
            but in great mercy I gather you up.
        In a burst of anger, I hid
            my face from you a moment,
        but in lasting kindness I love you.

    Said your redeemer, the LORD:
        This is to me like Noah's waters.
            As I swore
        Noah's flood would no more pass over the earth,
            so I have sworn off anger towards you, and rebuke.
        For the mountains may depart
            and the hills may shake,
        but my goodness does not depart from you,
            nor does my covenant of peace waver,
    said your beloved, the LORD.

    You poor, heart-battered, unconsoled:
    See, I set your walkways with mosaics,
        and founded you on sapphires,
        pile rubies atop your walls,
        hew gates from flaming garnet,
        mark all your borders with desire's stones,
    so all your children learn the Name
        and know great peace.
    Guide yourself with justice.
    Keep far from oppression, so you fear not,
        and from ruin, that it come not near you.

See, a stranger congregates without me:
    who musters against you, falls down before you.
See, I, even I, created a smith
    who blows on burning coals
    and draws forth a tool of his trade.
And I, even I, created a spoiler to destroy.
No weapon forged against you prospers, and
    every tongue roused against you, you condemn.
This is the portion of the Lord's servants
    and their justice from me—
God declares.

Yo, all who thirst: Come to water.
    And those without silver: Come.
Buy and eat. Yes, come. Buy wine and cheese
    without silver or price.
Why pay silver for no bread,
    and work unsatisified?
Listen: understand me, then eat well
    and delight your soul's self in plenty.
Incline your ear, and come to me.
    Hear, and your soul lives.

I make with you eternal covenant:
    surely David's goodness and mercy will follow.
See, I give him, a witness to peoples,
    a prince and messenger to nations.

OPENINGS

    See, you call to a nation unknown to you,
       and a people who knew you not
           run to you
  by dint of the LORD your God
       and holy One of Israel,
           who clarifies you.

ISAIAH 40:27-41:16
for LEKH LEKHA/לך־לך—Genesis 12:1-17:27

Why do you mutter, Jacob?
> or speak out, Israel:
> "My way is hidden from the LORD,
>> my case passed over by my God."

You do not know?
> You have not heard?

The God of forever—The LORD—
> the earth's Creator end-to-end—

never faints, never tires:
> no sounding out his reasons.

He gives power to the faint,
> and to the weak, more strength.

Even youths grow faint and tire,
> young men stumble down.

But those who wait upon the LORD spring up again:
> wings lift them like eagles.

They run and never tire,
> march on and do not faint.

Keep silent before me, O countries.
> The peoples renew their strength.

They approach now, they declare:
> Let us draw near together, to judgement.

Who roused a just one from the east
> and calls peoples to his feet?

Delivers nations before him
> and rules over kings?

OPENINGS

>   Gives them like dust to his sword,
>   like bent stubble to his bow?
>   He pursues them, he passes safely
>   on a path where his feet leave no trace.
>   Who made and did, who
>   calls to the generations from the beginning?
>   I, the LORD—the first
>   and to the last—I, He.
>   The countries see and fear.
>   Earth shakes from end to end:
>   they near, they come.
>   Each man helps his neighbor
>   and to his brother says, "Be strong."
>   The idol-maker urges on the goldsmith,
>   who hammers smooth plate on a form,
>   says of the joining, "Good!"
>   and fastens it with nails: it is not moved.
>
>   But you, Israel, my servant
>   Jacob, I chose you—
>   seed of Abraham my beloved
>   whom I took from the ends of the earth.
>   I called you from most distant parts.
>   I said to you, "You are my servant."
>   I chose you—I do not reject you.
>   Do not fear—for I am with you.
>   Don't dismay—I am your God.
>   I strengthen you—more, I support you;
>   more, I clasp you in my just right hand.

See ashamed and confounded all
    who raged against you;
come to nothing, they perish,
    those who oppose you.
Seek them, you won't find them.
    The men who strove with you
become like nothing—less than nothing—
    those who war against you.
For I the LORD your God
    hold your right hand.
I say to you, "Fear not.
    I help you."

Fear not, you worm, Jacob,
    you men of Israel.
I help you—
            says the LORD—
    your redeemer, the holy One of Israel.
See, I make you a new flail:
    a master of sharp teeth,
you will thresh the mountains, beat to dust
    and make hills like chaff.
You winnow them, and a wind lifts them up,
    and a whirlwind scatters them.
And you? You rejoice in the Name,
    glory in the holy One of Israel.

OPENINGS

ISAIAH 27:6-28:13 & 29:22-23
for SHEMOT/שמות—Exodus 1:1-6:1

In days to come, Jacob will take root, bud and blossom,
    and Israel's fruit fill the face of the world.

    Is he beaten like God beat his beaters?
        or, like he slays his slayers, is slain?
    In measure, when You cast her out, defend her—
his harsh breath removed her in the day of the east wind.
    So, by this Jacob's faults are atoned for,
        and this, the whole fruit:
    he casts off his sin
when he shatters all the altar stones like powdered chalk,
    so idols and pillars do not rise again.

    Yet the walled city, solitary,
is an abandoned home, forsaken like a wilderness.
    There a calf grazes,
and there he folds his knees and chews what sprouts.
    When branches dry, they break;
        women come and, with them, kindle fire.
For this, a people of no understanding,
    their Maker takes no pity on them.
    He who formed them shows no favor.

It happens. On that day the LORD will thresh them out
        from the Euphrates' branch to the Egyptian flood—
    and you, you will be gathered one by one,
        children of Israel.

It happens. On that day a great horn will sound,
    and those broken in the land of Assyria
    and those exiled to the land of Egypt
    will come and worship the unspoken Name
        in the holy mountain, in Jerusalem.

Ah! proud crown of Joseph's blessed second son
    (drunkards, fading flower of his splendid beauty)
    atop the head of a fruitful valley, crushed by wine—
See, my Lord has something strong and mighty.
    Like a hailstorm, terror, ruin,
as a gush of vast waters drowns he lays hand upon the earth,
so feet will trample the crowned pride of Ephraim's drunkards.
    And his splendid beauty's wilted flower
which tops the head of a lush valley
    becomes like the first fruit of summer
which the beholder sees and,
    while still in his hand, devours.
In that day the LORD of Hosts will be
    a crown of splendor and a morning glory
        for the remnant of his people,
    and a spirit of right for one who sits in judgment
    and might for those who turn back battle at the gate.
But even these reel with wine and stagger from liquor: priest
and prophet, ravished by liquor and swallowed by wine.
    Lost in the liquor, they take rapture for vision—
    judgment fouled like tables full of vomit.
        Crap. No clean place.

To whom would he teach knowledge?
And whom does he make understand?
    Those weaned off milk?
        Those yanked from the breasts?
    Like tat for tit, tit for tat,
        line for line, line by line,
            bit by bit, bit by bit?
So, through mockers' lips and in a strange tongue he speaks to this people to whom it was said:
    This is the resting place.
        You, give rest to the weary,
            and this, the refreshment.
But they would not hear. To them the word of the LORD is:
    tat for tit, tit for tat,
        line for line, line by line,
            bit by bit, bit by bit.
    So they walk and fall backward
        and are broken, and trapped, and taken.

That being so, the LORD who redeemed Abraham says this about the house of Jacob:
    Now Jacob is not ashamed,
    nor does his face blanch
when he sees his children—
    the work of My hand—
        in his midst.
    They keep My Name holy,
    and hallow the holy One of Jacob,
    and fear the God of Israel.

ISAIAH 6:1-7:6 & 9:5-6
for YITRO/יתרו—Exodus 18:1-20:23

In the year king Uzziah died, I saw the Lord seated on a high, raised throne:
    His train filled the temple. Seraphim stood about him with six wings—six wings to each one: two cover its face, two cover its feet, and with two it flies. And each called to the other, and said,
    "Holy, holy, holy LORD of Hosts,
        The whole earth full of his glory"
and the doorposts trembled at the caller's voice, and the house filled with smoke.
    Then I said:
    "Ah, me. I am undone—
        because I am a man of unclean lips
    and I dwell among a people of unclean speech—
        for my eyes have seen the King, the LORD of Hosts."
Then one of the seraphim flew to me, and in its hand a live coal, carried with tongs from off the altar, and it touched my mouth and said:
    "See, this has touched your lips
        and put away your fault, and atones for your sin."
And I heard my Lord's voice say:
    "I send whom? and who goes for us?"
And I said: "Here. I. Send me."
And he said:
    "Go, and tell this people:
    'You keep hearing, but you do not feel;
        you keep seeing, but do not understand.'

Make this people's heart fat
    and ears heavy and eyes shut,
lest their eyes see and their ears hear
    and their heart know, repent, and heal."
Then I said:
    "Until when, Lord?"
And he said: "Until
    when the cities lie waste without settlers
    and houses without man
    and the ground desolate waste,
and the One has removed mankind far away,
    and the heartland be mostly forsaken.
And more: if yet a tenth return,
    it is to burn again
like a felled elm or oak, a stump:
    the holy seed, a monument."

And it happened in the days of Ahaz son of Jotham son of Uzziah, king of Judah, that Rezin, king of Aram and Pekah son of Remaliah, king of Israel, went up to war against Jerusalem, but they could not prevail against it. When it was told to the house of David, saying, "Syria gives comfort to the Northern Kingdom," his heart and his people's heart trembled like forest trees shake facing the wind.

And the Name said to Isaiah: "Go now to meet Ahaz, you and your son 'A-remnant-returns', at the ditch's edge by the upper pool, near the felt-makers' field, and say to him:

"'Keep calm and be still. Fear not. Don't let your heart faint from these two stumps of smoking firebrands—the burning anger of Rezin and Aram, and of Remaliah's son.

"'Why? Because Aram devised evil against you? and Ephraim too—Remaliah's boy? saying, "Let us go up against Judah, and vex it, and divide it for ourselves, and set up a king in its midst—the son of 'any-God-is-good'."

"'For a child is born, for us—a son given to us—
   and authority rests on his shoulder
      and his name, pronounced
         "Wonderful-counsellor-mighty-champion-
            perpetual-father-general-peace"
   to increase rule of law and peace without end
      upon the throne of David, and upon his kingdom,
   to establish it and support it
      in justice and right, from now to forever.'"
The jealous LORD of Hosts does this.

OPENINGS

ISAIAH 43:21-44:23
for VA-YIKRA'/ויקרא—Leviticus 1:1-5:26

I formed this people for me.
    They recite my praise.
But you did not call me, Jacob.
    So, you tired of me, Israel?
You brought me no lambs for your burnt offerings,
    nor did your services honor me.
I don't require your sacrifice with grain,
    nor choke you with frankincense.
Your money bought no fragrant stalks for me.
    Your sacrificial fat does not fulfill me.
But you have weighed me down with your offenses.
    You tire me with your faults—
        I, even I—
who for my own sake blot out your transgressions.
    And your sins?
        I do not remember.

    Remind me.
Let us plead together.
    Recite, so that you may be cleared.
Your first father sinned
    and your teachers quarreled with me,
so I profane the keepers of the holy place
    and deliver Jacob to the curse,
    and Israel to reproaches.

Now hear, Jacob my servant
    and Israel, my chosen.
So says the LORD—
    who made you
        and formed you from the womb,
    who helps you—
Fear not, Jacob, my servant
    and upright one, whom I have chosen.
For I pour water on the thirsty,
    and streams on dry land pour my spirit on your seed,
    and my blessing on your children.
They spring up in the grass
    like willows beside streams of water.
One says "I" to the LORD.
Another calls in Jacob's name.
Another's hand writes "To the One"
    and takes the last name "Israel."

So, says the One—
    King of Israel and his near kinsman, LORD of Hosts—
        I first, I last, and without me, no God.
And who (like me) declares, explains, arranges
    (since I made people long ago)
        things to come, that come to pass?
        Let them rehearse it for me.
    Don't dread. Fear not.
    Did I not tell you long ago?
I announced to you, my witnesses:

Be there a god beside me?
No. Not a rock. Nothing.
   I know.

Fashioners of an idol, all of them are void,
   and their precious objects profit nothing.
Their own witnesses, they neither see nor know,
   so that they are confounded.
Who molds a god, or casts an idol without profit?
   Look. All his company are shamed.
      And artisans? The same.
   Assembled from dust, they all stand
      in awe, ashamed, together.
A smith forges an iron axe in coals
      and forms it with hammers,
      wrought by his strong arm.
   But he hungers, his strength fails.
   He drinks no water, and faints.
A woodcarver stretches out a line,
     traces in pencil,
     shapes with a chisel,
     and with a compass draws
     and makes the image of a man:
   beauty, like an Adam, to keep in a house.

Someone cuts down cedars,
    gets an elm or oak
    and takes the forest timber for himself.

He plants a fir. Rain makes it grow.
Wood is fuel for anyone,
    so he takes it and warms himself.
Also he burns it and bakes bread.
Also, he makes gods and bows to them,
    prepares idols and flops face-down before them.
Half he burns for fire.
    With that half he eats flesh:
        he roasts a roast and is stuffed.
Also, he warms himself and says, "Hah!
    I am warm. I see flame."
And what remains he makes into an idol, in his image.
    They fall down before it and worship
        and pray to it, and say,
        "Deliver me, because you are my god."

They neither know nor understand,
    since visions smear their eyes
        when pondering their hearts.
And none turns to his heart
    (wanting knowledge or insight), to say,
"Half of it I burned in fire.
    I even baked bread on its coals.
        I roasted flesh and ate.
    And I make what remains into a loathing?
        prostrate myself before a block of wood?"
Fed on ashes, a heart deceived turned him aside
    so he cannot save his soul,
        nor say, "There is no lie in my right hand."

OPENINGS

Remember these, Jacob
    and Israel, because you are my servant.
I formed you to serve me.
    Israel, I do not forget you.
Like darkness, I blot out your transgressions
    and like a cloud, your guilt.
Return to me, for I redeem you.

Sing out, heavens, for the LORD has wrought.
    Shout, deepest gorges of the earth.
The mountains break out singing,
    with woods and every tree in it,
because the Name, Jacob's near kinsman,
    clarifies Himself through Israel.

ISAIAH 1:1-27
for DEVARIM/דברים—Deuteronomy 1:1-3:22

A vision of Isaiah son of Amoz about Judah and Jerusalem, which he saw in the days of Uzziah, Jotham, Ahaz, and Hezekiah, kings of Judah:

> Hear, heavens.
> > Earth, lend an ear,
> > for the One has spoken:
> "Children.
> > I fed and raised them,
> > but they kick against me.
> An ox knows his master, an ass his owner's stall.
> > Does Israel know?
> > No.
> > My people don't think."

You nation gone missing, people
> laden, perverse, bad seed.

Spoiled children,
they abandon the Name, scorn the holy One of Israel.
> They turn away.
> > For what?

Beaten more, you revolt even more,
> all head-sick and heart-sore.

> From sole to crown, nothing sound:
wound and bruise, running sore not closed, not wrapped,
> unsalved with ointment.

OPENINGS

Your land: laid waste.
    Your cities: burned with fire.
Your husbandry: strangers devour it in your presence—
    a devastation, overthrown by strangers.
Yet Zion's daughter remains
    like a booth in a vineyard,
    like a hut in a cucumber patch,
    like a city besieged.
Had not the LORD of Hosts
    left a small remnant of us,
we would be, like Sodom,
    compared to Gomorrah.

Hear the word of the One, rulers of Sodom.
Lend your ears to our God's teaching, people of Gomorrah.
    "What are these great sacrifices to me?"
        says the One—
"I am glutted with burnt-offered rams and fatted calves;
    bulls' blood, lambs and he-goats do not move me.
    When you come to appear before me, who asks this—
        by your hand—to trample my courtyard?
Bring no more empty offerings.
    Incense disgusts me.
New moon and Sabbath, reading aloud—
    I cannot bear false worship, or assembly.
My soul hates your new moons and festivals.
    They become a burden to me
        I tire of bearing.

When you stretch out your hands
    I cover my eyes from you.
Also, though you pile up prayers,
    I do not hear.
Your hands are filled with blood.
    Wash.
    Be clear.
Put away your bad deeds from before my eyes.
    Stop doing evil.
    Learn to do good.
    Seek right.
Set the oppressed to rights.
    Defend the orphan.
    Plead for the widow.

"Come, now we argue together—"
    says the LORD—
    "if your crimes be like scarlet,
        they will be white as snow;
though bloodied crimson,
    they will be like wool.
If you will it, and hear
    you will eat the land's goodness.
But if you refuse and rebel,
    the sword devours you."
        God's mouth has spoken.

OPENINGS

How has she, a faithful city, turned a whore?
    Full of discretion, justice lodged with her,
        but now—assassins.
    Your silver turned to dross,
        your liquor cut with piss.
    Your princes—rebels
        and thieves' companions:
each one loves a bribe
        and solicits donations.
    They do not find for orphans;
nor does the widow's case come before them.

"Therefore,"
says the Master, LORD of Hosts, the mighty One of Israel,
"I take comfort from my enemies, and punish those I hate.

"Among you, I turn my hand again,
    and I refine your dross back into silver,
        pure and unalloyed.
And I return your judges to you, as in the beginning,
    and your counsellors, as at first.
After this,
    be called 'City of the Just'—
        a faithful city."

Zion: preserved through judgment and returned with justice.

CONSOLATIONS

ISAIAH 40:1-26
for VA-'ETHANNAN/ואתחנן—Deuteronomy 3:23-7:11

Comfort them, comfort my people—
    says your God—
speak to their heart, Jerusalem.
    Call to her
        now her trials are over,
        her guilt now pardoned,
for she has received, from the LORD's hand, double
    for all her sins.

A voice cries:
    In the wilderness, face
        the LORD's way,
    take a path through the desert
        straight to our God.
    Fill up every gorge,
        lay low every mountain and hill:
    the crooked make right,
        and the high ridges plain.
Splendor, the Name, is revealed
    and all flesh see as one—
        for God's mouth has spoken.

A voice says: Call!
    He said: What do I call?
All flesh? grass? and beauty like a wildflower?
    Grass withers, a flower fades
when God's breath blows upon it.

Truly, the people is grass—
    dried grass, faded flower—
but our God's word abides forever.

Go up on a high mountain,
    Zion. Preach.
Raise your voice with power.
    Preach, Jerusalem.
    Exalt, don't fear.
See, the LORD God comes in strength:
    his arm governs for him.
See, his wages are with him,
    and his labor before him.
Like a shepherd tends his flock,
    he gathers up lambs with his arm,
he cradles them close.
    He leads suckling dams.

Who measured waters in his palm
    and balanced the sky with spread fingers?
scooped the earth's dust,
    weighed the mountains on scales
        and hills with a balance?
Who measured the LORD's breath?
    Does a man teach him?
With whom did he consult? Who taught
    or drove him on the path of justice?
    taught him knowledge and made known
        the way of understanding?

Look: nations—a drop from a bucket—
    are reckoned like powder on scales.
Look: islands—dust, motes in a beam.
    And Lebanon? not enough kindling
        nor beasts enough for a burnt offering.

All the nations, like nothing before him,
    he reckons them not even waste.
And you compare God to whom?
    and he resembles what?
The image modeled by a craftsman,
    overlaid with gold leaf and forged silver chains?
The hollow offering:
    one chooses an unrotten tree
    and begs a cunning worker
        to make of it an unshakeable idol.

You do not know?
You do not hear?
You were not told from the beginning?
You do not feel the earth's foundation?

He abides beyond the earth's compass,
    its inhabitants like locusts.
He stretches sky like fine fabric
    spread out like a tent to dwell in.
He turns princes to nothing,
    makes judges of the earth like formless void.

Yet, unplanted
 yet, unsown,
 yet unrooted
  stems in earth—
He blows on them, they wither
 and wind whirls them off like straw.

You liken Me to whom? I equal what?
 says the holy One.
Raise your eyes on high.
 See who created these:
He brings forth countless hosts and numbers,
 calls on every one by name:
from great multitudes, of His own might,
 not one lacks.

CONSOLATIONS

ISAIAH 49:14-51:3
for 'EKEV/עקב—Deuteronomy 7:12-11:25

Zion said, "The Name has forsaken me;
    my lord has forgotten me."

Does a woman ignore her infant,
    or shun the son from her womb?
Yes, these may forget,
    but I, even I, do not forget you.
See, I have inscribed you on my palm,
    your walls forever before me.
Your children rush—
    your destroyers, your ravagers gone from you.
Lift your eyes, look around:
    assembled they all come to you.
I, I live—
        the LORD says—
you will wear them like ornaments,
    adorned like a bride.
Your ruins, your desolate land, ravaged, demolished
    now too cramped for those living there,
    even with those who devoured removed.

More. They say in your ears,
    those children born afterward:
"The place is too tight for me.
    Give me room to settle."

Then you say in your heart:
"Who has borne these to me?
I: bereft, barren,
an exile rejected—
and these: whose? raised how?
If I all alone remain,
then these, how come these?"

So— says the LORD God—
See: I raise my hand to the nations
and my banner to the peoples,
and they bring your sons on their laps,
and carry your daughters on their shoulders.
Kings will be your caretakers,
their queens your wet-nurses.
Noses to the earth they will bow to you,
will lick up the dust of your feet
and you will know that I am the One.
They are not ashamed who wait for me.

Is prey snatched from the grasp of the mighty,
or the innocent prisoner released?
But— so says the LORD—
yes, the tyrants' captives will be fetched back,
the spoils of terror redeemed.
And I, I myself will contend with your adversary;
even I will save your children.
I will feed your oppressors on their own flesh,
make them drunk on sweet wine, their own blood,
and all flesh will know

> that I the LORD saved you, redeemed you—
> I, The mighty One of Jacob.

So—   the LORD says—
where is the scroll of your mother's divorce,
> she whom I sent away?
Or to which of my lenders
> have I sold you?
Look, you were sold for your wrongdoings,
> and your mother cast out for your rebellion.
Why? I came—nothing, no one;
> I called—no one answered.
Is my hand too short to redeem?
> Or do I lack the strength to deliver?
Look: my rebuke dries the sea up,
> makes rivers wilderness—
> their fish stink from no water,
> and they die of thirst.
I clothe the heavens with blackness;
> make sackcloth to cover them.

My Lord the Name has given me
> the tongue of the learned
> to know, to sustain the weary
> > with words.
Morning to morning he arouses my ear
> to hear like the learned.
My Lord the Name opened my ear
> and I did not rebel,
> did not turn my back, or turn back.

My back I offered to the beaters,
    my cheeks to hair pluckers.
My face I hid not
    from insult and spittle.
My Lord the One helps me,
    so I am not confounded.
So I set my face like flint.
    I know no shame.

My defender is near.
    Who pleads against me?
        All rise.
Who is my adversary?
    Let him approach me.
Look. My Lord, the One, helps me.
    And he who condemns me?
Look: like worn-out clothing,
    a moth eats them.

Who among you fears the LORD?
Who listens to the voice of his servant
    who walks in darkness,
        nothing bright?
He trusts in the name of the LORD,
    and leans upon his God.
Look, all you who kindle fire,
    who wield torches:
depart in the flames of your fire,
    by the flares you ignited.

By my hand, this for you:
    where you lie down is terror.

Hear me, you who pursue justice,
    who seek the One:
Look to the rock you were hewn from,
    the pit where you were quarried.
Look to Abraham your father,
    and to Sarah who bore you.
Only one when I called him,
    I blessed him, and made him many.
For the Lord comforts Zion,
    comforts all her desolations.
He will make her wilderness like Eden,
    her desert like the LORD's garden.
Joy and pleasure are found in her,
    thanksgiving and the voice of song.

ISAIAH 54:11-55:5
for RE'EH/ראה—Deuteronomy 11:26-16:17

You poor, heart-battered, unconsoled:
See, I set your walkways with mosaics,
    and founded you on sapphires,
    pile rubies atop your walls,
    hew gates from flaming garnet,
    mark all your borders with desire's stones,
so all your children learn the Name
    and know great peace.
Guide yourself with justice.
Keep far from oppression, so you fear not,
    and from ruin, that it come not near you.

See, a stranger congregates without me:
    who musters against you, falls down before you.
See, I, even I, created a smith
    who blows on burning coals
    and draws forth a tool of his trade.
And I, even I, created a spoiler to destroy.
No weapon forged against you prospers,
    and every tongue roused against you, you condemn.
This is the portion of the Lord's servants
    and their justice from me—
        God declares.

Yo, all who thirst: Come to water.
    And those without silver: Come.
Buy and eat. Yes, come. Buy wine and cheese
    without silver or price.
Why pay silver for no bread,
    and work unsatisified?

Listen: Understand me, then eat well
    and delight your soul's self in plenty.
Bend your ear, and come to me.
    Hear, and your soul lives.
I make with you eternal covenant: surely,
    David's goodness and mercy will follow.

See, I give him, a witness to peoples,
    a prince and messenger to nations.
See, you call to a nation unknown to you,
    and a people who knew you not run to you
by dint of the LORD your God
    and holy One of Israel,
        who clarifies you.

ISAIAH 51:12-52:12
for SHOFETIM/שפטים—Deuteronomy 16:18-21:9

I, even I, am
    he, your comforter.

Who are you?
You fear one who dies,
    a son of man, made grass.
And you forget the One, your maker
    who stretched out the sky and founded earth
and tremble constantly, every day,
    at the oppressor's angry face
        made ready to destroy.
Yet where is the oppressor's rage?

A captive hurries toward the open,
    does not perish in the pit
        and does not want for bread,
for even I, the LORD your god,
    quiet the sea, its roaring waves—
        the LORD of Hosts, his name.
I put my words in your mouth,
    and my hand's shadow covers you,
to fasten the sky and make earth firm
    and say to Zion: You, my people.

    Wake up, wake up,
        get up, Jerusalem.
You drank his cup of wrath from the LORD's hand,

the reeling cup, drained to the dregs and sucked dry.
Of all her born children, not one to guide her,
    nor one to take her hand
    of all the children she has raised.
Alike, these befall you:
    (Now who will pity you?)
spoils and ruin, famine and the sword,
    (Who? Will I comfort you?)
your sons passed out in entryways on every street—snared
    like a wild ox in a net— full of the LORD's fury,
        of your God's rebuke.

    Now hear this,
    you afflicted ones drunk not on wine—
        so says your Lord, the Name, and your God
    (he defends his people)—
See, I take the reeling cup from your hand.
Drink no more dregs from the cup of my wrath.
I put it in the hand of your afflicters,
    who said to your soul:
Bow down, so we may pass over you
    and tread on your back like the earth,
    like a street, for those passing through.

    Awake. Awake.
    Put on your strength, Zion.
Wrap yourself in gorgeous cloth, Jerusalem, the holy city.
For no one ever enters you again uncircumcised, unclean.

Shake off the dust. Stand up.
   Take your ease, Jerusalem.
Loose the collar from your neck,
   Zion's captive daughter.

For,   so says the LORD,
you were sold for nothing, and are redeemed without silver.
   For so says the LORD God:
My people went down to Egypt first as strangers there, but
Assyrians oppress them without cause. And now, what have I here
      —God declares—
that my people is bought for nothing? Its rulers make them howl
      —God declares—
and constantly, every day, my Name is scorned.
Just as my people know my name, so surely on that day—
   I, the speaker—
      here am I.

   How pleasant.
On the mountains, the messenger's feet bring word of peace.
   The bearer of good news proclaims deliverance,
declares to Zion: Your God rules.

   Call!
Your watchmen raise the call, sing out as one.
Now they see eye-to-eye
   with the Name returned to Zion.
Break out, shout together, ruins of Jerusalem:
   the LORD comforts his people;
   he redeems Jerusalem.

The One flashes his holy arm
    in the eyes of all the nations,
and all ends of the earth will see
    the victory of our God.

    Away. Away.
    Get out of there.
    Touch no unclean thing.
Get out from her midst, and stay clear:
    you carry the LORD's instruments.
Take your leave without haste.
    Do not flee on the run.
The Name passes before you
    and gathers behind you,
        the God of Israel.

ISAIAH 54:1-10
for KI TETSE'/כי־תצא—Deuteronomy 21:10-25:19

Sing, you barren, childless.
> Break into song, cry out
>> who have not borne:
the children of abandoned wives
> outnumber children of the married.

The LORD said:
Enlarge your nomad campground, stretch
> the curtains of your dwelling out.
> Don't stint: extend your tent stays,
>> reinforce your stakes.
For right and left you burst forth,
> and your offspring inherits
nations, and peoples desolate cities.

Don't fear, don't feel ashamed,
> nor be confused, nor shoulder blame.
Forget your youthful shame,
> your widows' scorn recall no more.
For your husband is your Maker—
> The LORD of Hosts his name—
and your near kinsman, the holy One of Israel,
> called God of all the earth.

For, though a woman forsaken,
> a tortured spirit, the LORD called you.

Although a young wife cast aside,
    your God said:
In a small moment I forsook you,
    but in great mercy I gather you up.
In a burst of anger, I hid
    my face from you a moment,
but in lasting kindness I love you.

    Said your redeemer, the LORD:
This is to me like Noah's waters.
    As I swore
Noah's flood would no more pass over the earth,
    so I have sworn off
        anger towards you and rebuke.
For the mountains may depart
    and the hills may shake,
but my goodness does not depart from you,
    nor does my covenant of peace waver,
        said your beloved, the LORD.

ISAIAH 60:1-22
for KI TAVO'/כי־תבוא—Deuteronomy 26:1-29:8

Arise, shine, for your light has come,
    and the Name's glory risen over you.
Now look: darkness covers the earth
    and gloom clouds the peoples,
but the LORD shines upon you.
    His presence marks you.
Nations follow your light,
    and kings your clear dawn.

Lift your eyes, look about. See
    everyone gathered.
All come to you:
    your sons arrive from far away,
    your daughters borne on litters.
Then you see, reflect,
    and awe expands your heart.
Like the sea surges toward you,
    the nations' wealth comes to you.

Hordes of camels overwhelm you.
    Abraham's other sons all send
swift caravans from Sheba
    bearing gold and frankincense
    and herald praises to the LORD.
Bedouins herd all their flocks towards you.
    Ishmael's son's rams are served to you.

Offer them as welcome on my altar,
    when I adorn my house of beauty.

Who are these? Like clouds, they fly
    like pigeons to their windows.
The countries' vessels gather.
First, the ships of Tarshish
bring your children from distant ports
    with their silver and gold
in the name of the LORD your God,
    and for the holy One of Israel,
        who clarifies you.

Then a stranger's sons repair your walls.
    Also, their kings attend you.
For I struck you in my anger,
    but I love you at my pleasure.
Your gates open days on end
    and by night never shut
admit the wealth of nations,
    their kings leading the procession,
        for you.

For the people and the kingdom that do not serve you
    perish, and the nations lie waste.
Lebanon's bounty shipped to you all at once—
    cypress, pine and box-tree—
to adorn my sanctuary's home
    when I honor the place I rest my foot.

Your oppressors' sons enter bowed down to you,
>   and all your mockers,
>   stooped to the soles of your feet,
call you "City of the Name,
>   Stronghold of the holy One of Israel."

Where you became forsaken
>   and so hated none passed through,
I bestow on you a lasting dignity—
>   a joy to every age.
You nurse the nations' milk
>   and suck the teat of kings,
and know that I, the LORD, am your defender,
>   your redeemer, the mighty One of Jacob.

In place of the brass, I give gold;
>   for the iron I send silver
>   and instead of wood planks, brass,
>   and for stones, iron.
I make peace your overseers,
>   and justice your taskmasters.
Hear no more of violence in your land,
>   spoil or ruin at your borders,
but call your walls "Deliverance"
>   and your gates, "Praise."

You need no sun to light your days,
>   nor moon to shine for you
for the LORD is your constant light,
>   and you, God's ornament.

Your sun no longer sets,
    nor does your moon wax and wane
for the Name's become an ever-present light to you,
    and your days of mourning, peace.

Your people, all of them just,
    inherit the ancient land.
I make them beautiful:
    a shoot I have planted,
        the work of my hand.
The small one becomes a thousand,
    and the least a mighty nation:
I the LORD now quicken it, in time.

ISAIAH 61:10-63:9
for NITSAVIM/נצבים—Deuteronomy 29:9-30:20

    Rejoice.
    I rejoice in the Name.
    My soul whirls with my God.
Now he wraps me in safety's garments,
    he cloaks me with the robe of justice
like a groom puts on a turban
    or a bride adorns herself with jewels.
For as the earth brings forth her growth
    and as the garden sprouts seeds,
so the Lord, the One, makes justice and praise
    flourish in sight of all the nations.

For Zion's sake, I do not hush
    and for Jerusalem's I take no rest
until her justice shines through, radiant,
    and her triumph burns like a torch,
and nations see your justice
    and all kings your gravity,
and call you a new name
    pronounced by the LORD's mouth.
You are beauty's crown in the LORD's hand,
    a royal headdress in your God's palm.

No longer famous as forsaken,
    your land no more known by "desolate,"
you are called "My Delight in Her"
    and your land, "Espoused"

because the Name delights in you,
> married to your land.
As a youth marries a virgin,
> your sons espouse you.
With a groom's joy in a bride
> your God rejoices in you.

On your walls, Jerusalem,
> I have set watchmen:
all day, all night, always
> never still.
Recallers of the Name—
> no rest for you.
And you, give him no rest
> till he sets up
and makes Jerusalem
> a praise on earth.

The One has sworn by his right hand
> and his strong arm:
No more do I make your grain
> food for your enemies,
nor do strangers' sons drink your new wine,
> fruit of your labor.
Now reapers of it eat
> and praise the Name,
and those who press wine, drink it
> in my holy courts.

Pass on, pass on through the gates.
    Clear the people's way.
Raise and grade the highway free from stones,
    fly a banner for the peoples.
See, the One has proclaimed to the end of the earth:
    Say to Zion's daughter,
        "See, your rescue comes."
See his wages with him
    and his work before him.
And they call them "the holy people,"
    those near kinsmen of the LORD.
And they call you "Sought for," meaning
    "City not forsaken."

Who is this, come from Edom
    in red clothes, from the sheepfold?
This, proud in his garment,
    stooping in his great strength?
I am—
    speaking in justice—
        mighty to save.

How come your garments red
    and your clothes like tramped wine?
I tread the winepress alone.
    And from the peoples?
        No one with me.

I press them in my anger,
> trample them in my rage.
Their blood spatters my garments,
> and I stain all my clothes.

For the day of vengeance in my heart
> and the year of my close kinfolk
>> come.
I look, but none help;
> amazed, none support.
And so my own arm saves me.
> And my fury?
>> It sustains me.
I trample peoples in my anger,
> drunken them in my rage
and cast their blood down to the earth.

I recount the kindness of the Name,
> the LORD's praises,
for all that the One serves us,
> and for great good done the house of Israel
which he measures out with mercy,
> in harmony with his abundant kindness.
He said:
> They, my only people, children
>> do not lie.
So he preserves them.
> In all their trouble not a foe,

> but the angel of his presence
> > saved them.
> In his love and in his pity
> > he redeemed them,
> and he lifts them up and bears them
> > all the days of time.

OCCASIONS

ISAIAH 58:1-14
for YOM KIPPUR/יום כפור

Cry aloud, don't hold back.
    Raise your voice like a ram's horn.
Tell my people of their offenses,
    the house of Jacob of its sin.

Day-by-day they seek meaning,
    say they long to know my ways,
        like some nation that does right,
        and has not forsaken its God's laws.
    They desire righteous judgement.
    They wish that God were near:
"Why fast, if you do not see us?
    weigh our souls down, yet pay us no mind?"

Yet look! on your fast day you ply your affairs.
    You hunger, and pressure your workers.
See, you fast filled with strife and dispute,
    grasping guilt with clenched fists.
Today, such a fast will not make your voice heard on high.

    Is this, then, the fast I desire?
Made from dust you return to your soul for a day,
    and bow low your head like a bulrush,
    and lie down in sackcloth and ashes:
you call that a fast, an acceptable day to the LORD?

No. This is the fast I require:
    Strike off the chains of injustice.
    Cut loose the bonds of oppression.
    Set the yoked people free.
    You must break every yoke, every chain.

No. More.
    Share your bread with the hungry.
    Bring the homeless poor into your house.
    When you see naked ones, clothe them.
    Do not hide from your own flesh and blood.

Then your light shall break like dawn,
    and your wounds will heal themselves;
        justice will walk on before you,
    the Presence will track in your footsteps.
Then, when you call, one will answer.
    Cry out.
        One will say, "Here am I."

If you banish domineering from among you,
        finger wagging and mean-tempered speech,
    extend your own self to the hungry
        and attend the poor soul that's oppressed,
then your light will shine in darkness,
        and your dusk blaze like noon.
    The holy One will guide you always,
slake your dry soul in deserts, and strengthen your bones.
You will be like a watered garden,
    like the source of an unfailing spring.

Your children will raise the old ruins
    on foundations of past generations,
        and you shall be called
"Repairer of the breach, rebuilder of ways we can dwell in."

Sabbaths, if you turn your steps away from doing business
on my holy day, call Sabbath a delight, the Presence holy
    and honor it,
not going your own way,
    pursuing your own matters,
        talking talk,
then you will find delight in God,
    and I will set you astride the earth's high places,
    and feed you from the portion of your father Jacob.

    God's mouth has spoken.

ISAIAH 10:32-12:6
for PESACH VIII/פסח יום ח׳

Yet to this day the Assyrian stands on the northern heights and shakes his fist at Zion's daughter's mountain, the hill of Jerusalem.
>See, the master, LORD of Hosts
>>lops limbs with terror,
>
>hews the high and mighty,
>>lays the lofty low.
>
>He fells forest thickets with iron
>>so Lebanon, with majesty, falls.

But a shoot will sprout from the stock of Jesse
>and a branch from his root bear fruit;

and it will rest upon him:
>the spirit of the Name,
>a mind of wisdom and understanding,
>a spirit of counsel and might,
>a breath of knowledge and fear of the LORD.

His delight will be fear of the LORD,
>and he will not judge by appearance,
>nor condemn based on hearsay,

but he will govern the poor with justice,
>and plead fairly for the humble of the earth,
>and scourge earth with the rod of his mouth,
>and his lips' breath will snuff out the wicked.

Justice will gird his hips
>and steadiness his loins.

Then the wolf will abide among sheep,
    and the leopard will rest with the kid and the calf,
        the young lion and fat beeves, together—
    and a small child will lead them.
Cow and bear will graze in common—
    their young will lie down together—
    and a lion eat straw like an ox.
The infant will play by the adder's den
    and the toddler's hand reach in the viper's nest.
None will do evil, or destroy
    in all my holy mountain:
for the earth brims with knowledge of the LORD,
    like waters cover the sea.

And it will happen, on that day, that a root of Jesse will raise a signal for the people:
    nations will seek after him,
    and his consolation will be glory.
And it will happen on that day, that the Lord again sets his hand to redeem the remnant of His people who yet remain:
    from Assyria and from Egypt,
    from upper Egypt and Ethiopia
        and from Elam in Babylon,
    from Shinar between two rivers, from Fortress Syria,
        and from the islands of the sea.
He will raise a standard for the nations,
    gather outcast Israel, and assemble scattered Judah
        from the four quarters of the earth.

Ephraim's envy will end, and Judah's enemies will be cut off;
Joseph's fruitful son will not envy Judah
    and David's kingdom will not vex Ephraim.
Shoulder to shoulder, westward they swoop on the Philistines.
    They plunder the sons of the east,
        lay their hand upon Edom and Moab,
        and Ammon's children obey them.
The LORD will utterly destroy the tongue of the Egyptians' sea. He waves his hand over the River and, with his hot wind, splits it into seven stream beds, makes it passable dryshod.

And there will be a highway for the rest of His people, the remnant from Assyria, as there was for Israel, on the day they went up from the land of Egypt.

    And you will say on that day:
        Thank you, LORD.
    Although angry with me,
        your anger turned away
        and you comfort me.
    See, God, my salvation.
        I trust and dread not
    for my strength and my song, God
        the LORD, become my salvation.
    Draw water with joy
        from the spring of salvation.

You will say on that day:
    Praise the LORD, call in his name;
make known his deeds among nations,
    record how his name is on high.

Sing to the LORD for His excellent works,
    now known through all the earth.
Cry out and sing, you dwellers in Zion
    now—in your very midst the holy One—Israel.

ISAIAH 55:6-56:8
for SHABBAT ḤAZON/שבת חזון

Seek God when he is found,
    call him while he is near.
Let the bad one leave his way,
    the empty one his plots,
and turn to the LORD, who pities him.
    Our God does much to pardon.

For my plans are not your plots,
    nor your ways, my ways—
        the One declares—
as the sky above the earth,
    so my ways above your ways,
    my thoughts beyond your means.
Like the rain or the snow
    that falls from the sky
    does not just return,
    but first waters the earth,
    makes it yield and sprout
    and gives seed to the sower
    and bread to the eater,
so is my word that comes out from my mouth.
    It does not return to me empty,
    but does what I desire
    and nurtures what I sow.

So, begotten in joy,
    you bring forth in peace.

The mountains and hills break
> into song before you,
>> and all trees of the field clap hands.
Instead of the thornbush, a fir tree shoots forth
>> and in place of nettles, a myrtle:
it is, to the LORD, for a Name—
> a sign time-out-of-mind—
>> without end.

So—says the LORD—
> keep custom, and do right,
> for they bring my help near
> and reveal my right way.
How happy those who do,
> so that a child of man prevails,
> keeps from breaking Sabbath,
> keeps his hand's work from evil.

The stranger's son joined to the LORD must not say,
> "The One sets me apart from his people,"
nor the eunuch say,
> "See, I am a barren tree."
For here the LORD declares:
> The eunuchs who keep my Sabbaths
>> and choose what delights me
>> and hold fast to my covenant,
I give them a place in my house, inside my walls,
> and a name better than sons and daughters:
I give them a posterity
> that has no end.

And the strangers' sons who join the LORD
>   to wait on him, to love the Name
>   and be his servants?
All who keep from profaning Sabbath
>   and embrace my covenant,
I bring them to my holy mountain
>   rejoicing, in my house of prayer,
their burnt offerings and sacrifices
>   welcomed on my altar.
For my house is called a house of prayer for all the peoples—
>   says the LORD God,
>   gathering Israel's outcasts—
even more I gather to him,
>   beyond those now assembled.

ISAIAH 66:1-24
for SHABBAT ROSH ḤODESH/שבת ראש חודש

God says:
The sky is my canopy, and earth is my footstool.
Where would you build my house? Here?
   Is here where you mean me to rest?
My hand made all things, and all that will be—
   God declares—
yet I respect the humble, the afflicted spirit
   trembling at my word.

Slaughter an ox: kill a man.
   Sacrifice a lamb: strangle a dog.
      Offered grain? same as pig's blood.
         Burn incense: bless an idol.
These, who chose their own ways, their souls
   delight in their inventions,
so I choose to delude them, bring what they fear upon them.
Because I called, but no answer; I spoke, no one heard.
   They did evil in my sight,
and what they chose does not delight me.

Hear God's word, you who revere his word:
   Your hateful brothers cast you out for my Name's sake,
      and said,
"Let us glorify the Name, so we can see your joy."
   They will be shamed.
A roar from the city; a sound from the Temple:
   God's voice, paying out his foes.

Before she labored, she gave birth.
Before pain came, she delivered a male child.
Who has heard of this? Who seen such things?
    Does the earth bring forth in one day?
    Is a nation born at one stroke?
Yet Zion both labored and bore her children at once.
    Would I make the breach and not bear?
        says the One.
    Should I make birth yet hold back?
        says your God—
Rejoice with Jerusalem.
    Delight in her, all you who love her.
    Enjoy her joy, all you who mourn for her.
May you find succor, and feed at her breast.
    May you suckle delight from her glorious nipple.
Because—
    God says—
Behold: I extend to her peace like a stream
    overflowing banks, the wealth of nations.
You will nurse from it, ride high on a hip,
    and bounce upon knees.
Like a man's mother comforts him, I myself will comfort you
    and in Jerusalem you will be comforted.

Then you will see your hearts soar, your bones sprout like grass
    and God's hand will announce who serves him,
    and cry down his enemies.

Look there, the One comes in fire:
> His chariots whirlwind,
> his nostrils flared burning rebuke, flashing flame.
> By fire God judges, and all flesh by his sword.
> Those slain by the One will be many.

Those who consecrate and purify themselves, to enter secret gardens, one after another, eating pig's flesh, the unclean thing, the mouse, will perish together—
> God declares—
> so too their works and devices.
Even I will come to gather all the peoples, of all tongues; together they will come and see my glory. And I will put a sign among them.

Those who survive I will send out to the nations—to Tarshish, Pul and Lud (who draw the bow), Tubal and Javan, to distant shores that have not heard a rumor of my Name, nor seen my glory—where they will tell my glory to the nations. And they will bring all your brothers out from all the nations: an offering to the One—on horseback and in chariots, in litters, riding mules and swift camels—to my holy mountain, Jerusalem,
> God says,
like the children of Israel bring grain in a clean vessel to God's house. And some among them I will take as priests and Levites,
> says the LORD.

For just like the new heavens and new earth which I make stand
before me—
    God declares—
    so will your seed and name endure.
And it shall be, from new moon to new moon,
    from Sabbath to Sabbath
all flesh will come to worship before me,
    says the LORD.
And they will go out and see
    the corpses of those men who rebelled against me.
The worm that eats them will not die,
    nor will the fire that consumes them be extinguished,
    and they will be horror to all flesh.

And it shall be, from new moon to new moon,
    from Sabbath to Sabbath
all flesh will come to worship before me,
    says the LORD.

SOURCES

The Bible: Authorized King James Version with Apocrypha, Oxford University Press

Biblia Hebraica: Stuttgartensia

Blenkinsopp, Joseph
Isaiah 1-39, Anchor Bible 19
Isaiah 40-55, Anchor Bible 19A
Isaiah 56-66 Anchor Bible 19B, Doubleday

Brown-Driver-Briggs, *Hebrew and English Lexicon*, Hendrickson Publishers

Hebrew-English Tanakh, Student Edition, Jewish Publication Society

Hertz, J. H., *The Pentateuch and Haftorahs: Hebrew Text, English Translation and Commentary*, Soncino Press

Rashi, *Pentateuch and Rashi's Commentary: A Linear Translation Into English*, tr. Abraham Ben Isaiah and Benjamin Sharfman, SS&R Publishing Company

ALSO BY LAURANCE WIEDER

After Adam: The Books of Moses, Highland Books, 2019

PoemSite: Songs in the Landscape, Omerta Publications, 2015

Perek Shirah: A Chapter of Song, Omerta Publications, 2013

Words to God's Music: A New Book of Psalms, Eerdmans, 2003

The Poets' Book of Psalms, Oxford, 1999; HarperCollins, 1995

The Red Sea Haggadah, Wiseacre Books, 1995

Chapters into Verse: Poetry in English Inspired by the Bible,
2 volumes (with Robert Atwan), Oxford, 1993

The Last Century: Selected Poems, Picador Poetry/
Pan/MacMillan Australia, 1992

Duke: The Poems as told to Laurance Wieder, Wiseacre Books, 1990

No Harm Done, Ardis, 1975

The Coronet of Tours, Ithaca House, 1972

www.ingramcontent.com/pod-product-compliance
Lightning Source LLC
Chambersburg PA
CBHW060501080526
44584CB00015B/1509